THE
TROUBLE
WITH
REALITY

⇄

A Rumination on
Moral Panic in Our Time

BROOKE GLADSTONE

WORKMAN PUBLISHING · NEW YORK

To Fred, Maxine, and Sophie

Copyright © 2017 by Brooke Gladstone

All rights reserved. No portion of this book may be reproduced—
mechanically, electronically, or by any other means, including
photocopying—without written permission of the publisher.
Published simultaneously in Canada by Thomas Allen & Son Limited.

Library of Congress Cataloging-in-Publication Data is available.

ISBN 978-1-5235-0238-7

Design by Janet Vicario

Workman books are available at special discounts when purchased in
bulk for premiums and sales promotions as well as for fund-raising or
educational use. Special editions or book excerpts can also be created
to specification. For details, contact the Special Sales Director
at the address below, or send an email to specialmarkets@workman.com.

Workman Publishing Co., Inc.
225 Varick Street
New York, NY 10014-4381
workman.com

WORKMAN is a registered trademark of Workman Publishing Co., Inc.

Printed in the United States of America
First printing April 2017

10 9 8 7 6 5 4 3 2 1

Doubt is to certainty as neurosis is to

psychosis. The neurotic is in doubt and

has fears about persons and things; the

psychotic has convictions and makes claims

about them. In short, the neurotic has

problems, the psychotic has solutions.

—Thomas Szasz, *The Second Sin*

IN HERE

Perhaps you picked up this book because an icy hand grips your viscera; sometimes squeezing, sometimes easing, always present. And you suspect that this intimate violation, this forced entry, proceeds from something more profound than politics. You imagine that reality itself is engaged in an epic existential battle and you stand helpless against the onslaught, as the truth is trumpled into dust.

That said, you can feel better. After reading this, perhaps that terrible pressure will begin to ebb, but it will never leave you. Having watched history unspool in a direction you never believed it could go, now you question reality, and it's likely you always will. Because reality is more slippery than a pocketful of pudding.

Is reality what we are able to confirm with our five senses? As *New Scientist* magazine noted some years back, "This answer ignores such problematic entities as electrons, the recession and the number 5," not to mention a heap of phantom limbs.

Is reality what a significantly large group of people hold to be true? Certainly no one currently living in America (or on Earth) could believe that. Now the unknowing or unhinged can coalesce a vast number of like-minded souls into a force so powerful it can shift reality's prism or elect a president.

Part of the problem stems from the fact that facts, even a lot of facts, do not constitute reality. Reality is what forms after we filter, arrange, and prioritize those facts and marinate them in our values and traditions.

Reality is personal.

⇆

America's most determined architect and annihilator of reality was the science fiction master Philip K. Dick. Included in the anthology *The Shifting Realities of Philip K. Dick* is a speech he delivered in 1978:

> "It was always my hope, in writing novels and stories which asked the question 'What is reality?,' to someday get an answer...."

Even after writing over thirty novels, he never found one. Finally, when a philosophy student asked him to define reality, he replied:

> "'Reality is that which, when you stop believing in it, doesn't go away.' That's all I could come up with."

But he knew we urgently needed a better answer:

"... because today we live in a society in which spurious realities are manufactured by the media, by governments, by big corporations, by religious groups, political groups.... Very sophisticated people using very sophisticated electronic mechanisms. I do not distrust their motives; I distrust their power. They have a lot of it. And it is an astonishing power: that of creating whole universes, universes of the mind. I ought to know.... It is my job to create universes.... And I have to build them in such a way that they do not fall apart two days later.

"... the matter of defining what is real— that is a serious topic, even a vital topic. And in there somewhere is the other topic, the definition of the authentic human. Because the bombardment of pseudo-realities begins to produce inauthentic humans very quickly—as fake as the data pressing at them from all sides. Fake realities will create fake humans. Or, fake humans will generate fake realities and then sell them to other humans, turning them, eventually, into forgeries of themselves. . . . It is just a very large version of Disneyland."

What Dick saw forty years ago many of us see now, at least those of us whose reality embodies liberal values. It was as if *that* reality was sucked into a black hole, which then erupted, spewing hot flows of a grimmer vision. No American escaped the tremors—many enjoyed them—but more than half the nation suffered some degree of vertigo.

What to do? Often, the graver the illness, the harsher the treatment.

⇆

If fake reality is the problem, the logical first step is to track it to its source, but that is a very short, very frustrating expedition, because fake reality begins at home. In your head. And even before that, in your *umwelt*.

Umwelt expresses the idea that different animals living on the same patch of earth experience utterly disparate realities. Writing in *Edge*, neuroscientist David M. Eagleman put it this way:

> "In the blind and deaf world of the tick, the important signals are temperature and the odor of butyric acid. For the black ghost knifefish, it's electrical fields. For the echolocating bat, it's air-compression waves.
>
> "The small subset of the world that an animal is able to detect is its *umwelt*.
>
> "The bigger reality, whatever that might mean, is called the *umgebung*.

"To appreciate the amount that goes undetected in our lives, imagine you're a bloodhound dog. Your long nose houses two hundred million scent receptors . . . your wet nostrils attract and trap scent molecules. The slits at the corners of each nostril flare out to allow more airflow . . . your floppy ears drag along the ground and kick up scent molecules. Your world is all about olfaction."

One day while trotting behind your master, you are stunned by a revelation. The human with whom you stroll is profoundly disabled! You glory in smell while he stumbles along with stunted senses! How diminished, how sad, his life must be.

"Obviously, we suffer no absence of smell because we accept reality as it's presented to us. Without the olfactory capabilities of a bloodhound, it rarely strikes us that things could be different."

Therein lies the root of the problem, succinctly rendered by the philosopher Arthur Schopenhauer in his aptly titled *Studies in Pessimism*: "Every man takes the limits of his own field of vision for the limits of the world."

⇄

We cannot know the world, but we have to live somewhere. So we construct cozier, more comprehensible versions, move in and hunker down. Meanwhile, out there in the *umgebung*, millions of others do likewise, people we don't know and mostly don't care to. These people are stereotypes.

Journalist and critic Walter Lippmann introduced stereotypes, in the psychological sense, back in the 1920s. In his seminal work *Public Opinion*, he noted that we pick up a salient detail about a person or group—black, white; international banker, kindergarten teacher; in Brooklyn, Baton Rouge—and then blithely fill in the rest of the blanks. Now we think we know them.

Our worldview is built on a bedrock of stereotypes, not just about people but also about the way things work. The power of those stereotypes—vital to survival in this unfathomable world—is as profound as it is inescapable.

Stereotypes, Lippmann wrote, focus and feed on what is familiar and what is exotic, exaggerating each in the process: "The slightly familiar is seen as very familiar and the somewhat strange as sharply alien." They are refreshed continually, both by close observation and false analogy.

True or not, they carve neural pathways, sluices that stem the torrent of conflicting impressions and ideas churning through the *umgebung*.

In the end, stereotypes create the patterns that compose our world. It is not necessarily the world we would like it to be, he says, it is simply the kind of world we expect it to be.

"We feel at home there. . . . We are members. . . . And though we have abandoned much that might have tempted us before we creased ourselves into that mould, once we are firmly in, it fits as snugly as an old shoe.

"No wonder, then, that any disturbance of the stereotypes seems like an attack upon the foundations of the universe. It is an attack upon the foundations of *our* universe, and, where big things are at stake, we do not readily admit that there is any distinction between our universe and the universe."

It stands to reason that if such a disturbance can endanger our universe, our own stereotypes can wreak terrible havoc on the universes of others. How could they not? The purpose of stereotypes is to filter, to *shrink* our field of vision. So they give rise to vast blind spots that inevitably lead to smash-ups when worlds collide.

Case in point: Looking back at America before the First World War, Lippmann observed that one of America's core "stereotyped" ideas was that technological development was synonymous with progress. All evidence to the contrary was channeled off. He described what followed:

"They saw the expansion of cities, but not the accretion of slums. . . . They expanded industry furiously at reckless cost to their natural resources; they built up gigantic corporations without arranging for industrial relations. They grew to be one of the most powerful nations on earth without preparing their institutions or their minds for the ending of their isolation.

"They stumbled into the World War morally and physically unready, and they stumbled out again, much disillusioned, but hardly more experienced."

After the war, many of the nation's highest ideals were shipwrecked along with the shattered stereotypes, leaving an entire generation adrift. We pay a high price to live in our gated realities.

$$\rightleftarrows$$

Stereotyping is like eating, an act essential to our well-being. And like eating, there is an unhealthy tendency to overindulge. For this disorder, there are no sure cures, and most treatments are deeply unpleasant.

It is a nauseating enterprise, tinkering with your universe. You could break it.

But what if you have no choice? You know what happens; you've done it. We've all done it. In a 1906 lecture, pragmatist William James described exactly what transpires when suddenly a person's trusty stock of old opinions is imperiled. The reason can vary; maybe it's because the facts contradict them, or they contradict each other, or they are getting in the way of what he wants. No matter, the result is always a deep and strange unease, which can be escaped only by modifying one's previous opinion.

"He saves as much of it as he can, for in this matter of belief we are all extreme conservatives. So he tries to change first this opinion, and then that . . . until at last some new idea comes up which he can graft upon the ancient stock with a minimum of disturbance of the latter. This new idea is then adopted as the true one. It preserves the older stock of truths with a minimum of modification, stretching them just enough to make them admit the novelty, but conceiving that in ways as familiar as the case leaves possible. . . .

"The most violent revolutions in an individual's beliefs leave most of his old order standing. Time and space, cause and effect, nature and history, and one's own biography remain untouched. New truth is always a go-between, a smoother-over of transitions. It marries old opinion to new fact so as ever to show a minimum of jolt, a maximum of continuity."

You alter only what you must to avoid collateral damage to the code you live by. To do otherwise would both deny you serenity and defy your biochemistry. It's behavior bred in the bone, and the blood, and the brain.

Consider the experiment conducted by Emory University professor Drew Westen in 2006. He used fMRI brain scans to monitor what happens inside a voter's head when confronted with candidates' statements that showed lying or pandering.

As he described in an *On the Media* interview, voters in the study reckoned easily with the incriminating statements of the *opposing* candidate. But when they confronted hypocrisy from their *own* candidate . . .

WESTEN: The first thing that is activated were a series of negative emotion circuits that were basically—for any of your listeners who can remember *Lost in Space*, it was "Will Robinson, danger, danger." They saw danger. They saw a threat, and you could see it all over their brain. Then you saw activation in the part of the brain called the anterior cingulate. It monitors and deals with conflict. So they were in conflict . . . to figure a way out. And then, after they had come to their conclusion that there was really no problem for their guy, you saw activation in parts of the brain that are very rich in the neurotransmitters involved in reward. These are the circuits in the brain that get activated when junkies get their fix.

ME: You mean once they figured out how best to lie to themselves, they got a blast of oxytocin or something?

WESTEN: [*laughs*] Very, very close, that's right. So they got this huge blast of dopamine, which is involved in reward.

ME: In other words, the same thing you get when you take coke.

WESTEN: That's exactly right. There was no reasoning at all going on.

That is what you're up against. Who would choose violation over validation? The very wiring of your mind and body rebels against that choice. Yet any sincere reckoning with reality demands that you strain, violently, against the natural, lifelong limitations of your *umwelt*, or as neuroscientist David Eagleman proposes, at least accept the idea that the *umwelt* exists.

"I think it would be useful if the concept of the *umwelt* were embedded in the public lexicon. It neatly captures the idea of limited knowledge, of unobtainable information, and of unimagined possibilities. Consider the criticisms of policy, the assertions of dogma, the declarations of fact that you hear every day—and just imagine if all of these could be infused with the proper intellectual humility that comes from appreciating the amount unseen."

Especially in treacherous times. In Ursula K. Le Guin's *Left Hand of Darkness*, a human envoy confronts a species locked in a cold war, whose customs and biology are confoundingly strange. His enigmatic guide muses, "To learn which questions are unanswerable, and *not to answer them*: this skill is most needful in times of stress and darkness."

The patience to defer judgment—that's a start, but probably not why you picked up this book. If you are human, while you may have some concern for the chaos within, those icy fingers are pulsing in Morse code that there is a bigger problem *out there*.

OUT THERE

To ease the transition from the world within to the world out there, cast one last look inward and consider that, after all, we are what we eat.

In 1985, critic and educator Neil Postman published *Amusing Ourselves to Death*, the most incisive, impassioned warning label ever issued on our media diet. To illuminate the danger, he contrasts two pivotal works of dystopian fiction: George Orwell's *1984* and Aldous Huxley's *Brave New World*.

In Orwell's vision, he notes, we are crushed by a merciless oppression imposed by others, whereas in Huxley's vision, we are seduced, sedated, and satiated. We enslave ourselves.

"What Orwell feared were those who would ban books. What Huxley feared was that there would be no reason to ban a book, for there would be no one who wanted to read one. Orwell feared those who would deprive us of information. Huxley feared those who would give us so much information that we would be reduced to passivity and egoism.

"Orwell feared that the truth would be concealed from us. Huxley feared that the truth would be drowned in a sea of irrelevance. Orwell feared that we would become a captive culture. Huxley feared that we would become a trivial culture, preoccupied with some equivalent of the feelies, the orgy porgy and the centrifugal bumblepuppy.

"In 1984, Orwell added, people are controlled by inflicting pain.

"In *Brave New World*, they are controlled by inflicting pleasure. In short, Orwell feared that what we hate will ruin us. Huxley feared that what we love will ruin us. . . ."

Orwell, who in 1948 was fixed on Nazi devastation and Soviet ascendancy, seemed to have nailed it. But thirty-seven years later, Postman saw that in our time and place, it's unquestionably Huxley. He portrayed a world that leads ineluctably to the election of Donald Trump.

⇆

Trump's campaign rhetoric pumped out endless streams of comedy and melodrama, apocalypse and deliverance, bitterness and bullshit. To some, it was enthrallingly frank. To others, Trump's victory did not merely subvert America's core values, it shattered their worldview. The codes more than half the nation devised to interpret the world, the channels they carved to divert the flow of incompatible ideas, collapsed.

What stereotypes were busted by Trump? Mostly, they pertain to our deep-rooted belief in the infallibility of our democracy, though some of those stereotypes were formed long before our nation was born.

English poet John Milton, famed for the seventeenth-century epic *Paradise Lost*, spent years as defender-in-chief for Oliver Cromwell in a convulsive time. He penned a ferocious polemic to Parliament against censorship, declaring, *Let Truth and Falsehood grapple! In a free and open encounter, Truth will win.*

> "Lords and Commons of England, consider what Nation it is whereof ye are . . . a Nation not slow and dull, but of a quick, ingenious, and piercing spirit, acute to invent, subtle and sinewy to discourse, not beneath the reach of any point the highest that human capacity can soar to."

His speech, called "Areopagitica," inspired and heartened America's founding fathers, especially Thomas Jefferson:

"Truth is great and will prevail if left to herself . . . she is the proper and sufficient antagonist to error, and has nothing to fear from the conflict . . ."

Oh, come on.

The laws of human nature do not provide for the triumph of reason. History and the internet have lavishly demonstrated that this notion, this stereotype, is false. But that cold truth stands in brazen defiance of the code that rules our world and the laws that govern our country.

First among them is the First Amendment, which exists because the founding fathers were convinced that wisdom emerged from information. They codified civil liberties to ensure that our speech and our press were free.

It was a beautiful notion, and like many pristine ideas, unsullied by grubby reality, both because we instinctively resist unwelcome information and because the press cannot be the sole guarantor of reason. As Walter Lippmann observed, the press is, and always has been, a business, and one that the people only grudgingly support.

"We expect the newspaper to serve us with truth however unprofitable the truth may be."

Here, Lippmann's volume seems to rise. He is, after all, a newspaperman. He decries the critics who rebuke the media for not holding to the same standards as a school or a church. He says the widespread idea that the press can serve as a public institution without public support is not just untenable, it plainly illustrates "the concave nature of democracy."

Citizens may recoil from paying for the news, he noted, because they see it as a natural right. But in the absence of consumer coin, the media must be fueled by advertisers seeking consumers and investors pursuing profit. Novelty and drama pay to keep the presses rolling, and so the "news" that supposedly informs reason becomes the dog wagged by its own tail.

"If the newspapers, then, are to be charged with the duty of translating the whole public life of mankind, so that every adult can arrive at an opinion on every moot topic, they fail, they are bound to fail, in any future one can conceive they will continue to fail."

Lippmann says the press must share the blame for that, because like the rest of us, it bought into the myth that it *can* in fact fix what ails us.

"It has . . . encouraged a democracy, still bound to its original premises, to expect newspapers to supply spontaneously for every organ of government, for every social problem, the machinery of information which these do not normally supply themselves. Institutions . . . have become a bundle of 'problems,' which the population as a whole, reading the press as a whole, is supposed to solve."

And yet in America's earliest days, much of the press *was* fully engaged in vigorous debate over the serious business of nation building, fulfilling the founders' mission. But by the 1830s, when author James Fenimore Cooper returned home to upstate New York after several years in Europe, his fresh eyes saw a press brought low by greed.

> ". . . [W]hile the contest was for great
> principles, the press aided in elevating the
> common character . . . and maintaining the
> common interests . . .
>
> ". . . but since the contest has ceased and the
> struggle has become one purely of selfishness
> and personal interests, it is employed as a
> whole, in fast undermining its own work,
> and in preparing the nation for some terrible
> reverses, if not in calling down upon it, a just
> judgment of God."

In *The American Democrat*, he cranks up the fire and brimstone.

"As the press now exists, it would seem to be expressly devised by the *great agent of mischief*, to depress and destroy all that is good, and to elevate and advance all that is evil in the nation."

The press is thus a tool, doing work that would please the devil. But in Cooper's scenario, the devil himself is described. He is "the demagogue." That lands us at the source of your anxiety and our reality trouble. So let's break that down.

⇆

Michael Signer, author of *Demagogue: The Fight to Save Democracy from Its Worst Enemies*, wrote that true demagogues must meet four criteria proposed by Cooper: They must pose as a mirror for the masses; ignite waves of intense emotion; use that emotion for political gain; and break the rules that govern us.

Enter Donald Trump, gasbag billionaire, reality-TV hotshot, invincible ratings rocket. Stressed by shrunken audiences and revenue, the media are willing marks for a candidate their own pundits variously describe as a "carnival barker," a "crackpot," "the biggest goofball ever to enter the Oval Office Sweepstakes," and a "tire fire in an expensive suit."

Trump knew better, as he himself explained in his 1987 book, *The Art of the Deal*:

> "The final key to the way I promote is bravado. I play to people's fantasies. People may not always think big themselves, but they can still get very excited by those who do. That's why a little hyperbole never hurts. People want to believe that something is the biggest and the greatest and the most spectacular."

Before the 2016 election, Signer wrote that for a long time he was reluctant to label Trump a demagogue because he didn't mirror the masses or threaten the rules of governance.

"But when he began openly posturing as a mirror of the masses and courting unlawfulness and even violence, I concluded that he had, in fact, become a demagogue, which meant that he also crossed the line into a clear Constitutional danger zone, according to the Founding Fathers."

Meanwhile, we laughed and laughed, opponents and supporters alike, for the same reason: because he violated, profusely and with brio, traditional norms of political and civil discourse.

Trump's supporters, who felt increasingly anxious or displaced in the prevailing consensus reality, could see what was happening. But those of us who were relatively at ease—our field of vision was obstructed. So we scoffed and mocked as Trump put a half nelson choke hold on reality.

But *how* did he do it? Some historians suggest he followed an authoritarian playbook largely written in the last century. But before serving up that anatomy, another question must be addressed.

⇄

Was Trump's rise part of a brilliantly executed secret plan? A *conspiracy*?

As I write this, and most likely, as you read this, that is unknown. Historians are still arguing about Hitler.

What *is* known, when grappling with the greased pig of reality, is that research suggests voters whose candidates *lose* are more likely to embrace conspiracy theories. And this is a bipartisan phenomenon.

Political scientists Christina Farhart, Joanne Miller, and Kyle Saunders polled Republicans and Democrats before and after Trump's election. They found that the percentage of Republicans who generally agreed that shadowy cabals were running things dropped from 28 to 19 percent. For Democrats, the number *rose*, from 27 to 32 percent.

Does that mean liberals and conservatives confront conspiracy theories in the same way? Not necessarily. Researchers at UCLA found conservatives more likely than liberals to believe conspiracy theories, especially apocalyptic ones. This finding was reflected in their bodies, too: Conservative hearts raced faster in response to threatening stimuli than liberal ones.

On the other hand, that study was conducted while Barack Obama was well into his second White House term, so the conservatives may have been primed, having already suffered long years of dread.

Even Trump's victory has not loosened conspiracy's grip on his supporters. It remains a vital part of his message and, given the ferocity of his foes, a persuasive one. Conspiracy will always fortify mindsets, and because our worldview relies on a web of beliefs, it follows that one distortion will lead to another, and another.

Example: In 2012, Australian psychologist Stephan Lewandowsky reported on a survey of more than a thousand readers of climate blogs and found that strong belief in the free market was correlated with climate change denial. *And* denial that HIV causes AIDS. *And* denial that smoking causes cancer. Deny science, protect the free market, preserve the web.

That's why *liberals* favor the conspiracy theory that Russia is the reason Donald Trump is president. It aligns with the liberal code: It is impossible that one such as Trump could arise spontaneously in our exemplary democracy. His victory *required* Vladimir Putin.

Journalist Masha Gessen cut her teeth reporting in her native Russia, but has long worked in the United States. In a series of penetrating articles in *The New York Review of Books*, she tried, in vain, to prepare its readers (and her journalist colleagues) for Trump's likely election. She also spoke to *On the Media* after the election.

GESSEN: . . . most Americans and the media certainly didn't believe that there was even a possibility that Donald Trump would be elected president. And I think part of the reason for that disbelief was an inability to look around . . . and consider the possibility that the United States is part of a worldwide trend . . . of right-wing populists coming to power. . . . If we looked at European elections, European democracies falling like dominoes at this point . . . I'm not saying there are exact parallels, but there are always lessons to be learned from what's happening elsewhere.

ME: You think the media have totally missed the point. You wrote, "Imagine that your teenage child has built a bomb and has just set it off in your house. The house is falling down all around you and you're blaming the neighbor's kid who threw a pebble at your window." So Trump's the kid with the matches and Putin's the kid with the pebble?

GESSEN: [*laughs*] Yes. And the thing is, you know, your kid is still in the basement and now he's building something even bigger— whereas the neighbor's kid, he just runs around the neighborhood throwing pebbles in everybody's window. I mean, we know he does that.

What is fascinating to me is sort of the psychology of this desire to "other" the threat. It's a very American thing to do. Somehow it becomes a little bit easier mentally to live with if it's other people.

ME: So you think that's why the Putin–Trump connection is such an attractive narrative for the media?

GESSEN: I think so. It . . . sounds credible, and I also think that we in the media have a very difficult time using big, scary words, for good reason. When the time has come to use the [term] "homegrown fascist," which is actually the only kind that there is, we have a very hard time doing that. So this is a different way of communicating how terrifying we're finding Trump. But it's a bad way. It prevents us from seeing just how dire a threat Trump is.

So it follows that the wisest course is to approach conspiracy theories with extreme caution, because we are all primed to find an explanation that preserves our web. Evidence-based conclusions and baseless assumptions become inextricably intertwined.

⇄

Now back to the reality "out there" and its discontents. Where were we?

Ah, yes. Trump's canny use of the demagogue's playbook, beginning with Cooper's prescription that one must serve as a mirror to the masses. Trump's mirror did not present a pretty picture, but to those who saw themselves reflected there, it offered the deep relief of validation. It was a mirror reflecting loss, righteous anger, and future redemption. And Trump held it high, on every podium and platform, and even from the prow of the battleship USS *Iowa* in Los Angeles in September 2015:

> *"The 'silent majority,' believe me, is back, and . . . I don't think we have to call it a silent majority anymore, because they're not silent.*
>
> *"They're disgusted with our incompetent politicians.*
>
> *"They're disgusted with the people who are giving our country away. . . .*
>
> *"They're disgusted when a woman who's nine months pregnant walks across the border, has a baby, and you have to take care of that baby for the next eighty-five years.*
>
> *"They're disgusted by what's happening to our country. And . . . you're going to remember who the people are that are here, because we're doing something special.*

"This is a movement. We're going to make our country great again—believe me. We will make our country great again."

Trump said he wanted to "take the system apart." And throughout, he fingered those responsible for all that disgust some of us felt: the Muslims, the Hispanics, the blacks. And, by way of his white supremacist supporters, whom he took pains to neither recognize nor disavow, the Jews.

The definite article—*the*—reduced millions, even billions of people to a unitary mass with a single ideology and a single goal: to push us aside and take what we'd believed would always be ours.

As for women, he loved them, in his fashion:

". . . the only difference between me and the other candidates is that I'm more honest and my women are more beautiful."

"Grab them by the pussy. You can do anything."

To be sure, Cooper's prescription that demagogues seek to engage the masses and inspire emotion includes goals shared by every ambitious politician. The question is, what kind of emotion?

The fact that Trump was not damaged by his frank celebration of sexual assault points to what he had unleashed. Permission to speak hateful thoughts is a spur to act on them. When his campaign events were disrupted, he cheered on the violence. As protesters were being removed from a St. Louis rally, Trump complained about how long it was taking. He said the country needed to "toughen up."

"You know, part of the problem and part of the reason it takes so long is nobody wants to hurt each other anymore, right?"

In August 2015, two Boston men saw a homeless Mexican immigrant sleeping outside a commuter rail station, beat him with a metal pipe, punched and urinated on him, and gleefully walked off. Upon their arrest, one of them told the police,

"Donald Trump was right. All these illegals need to be deported."

Trump said the attack was a shame, but perhaps not a crying shame, because the goons' motives were pure.

"I will say that people who are following me are very passionate. They love this country and they want this country to be great again."

The Southern Poverty Law Center reported that in the run-up to the election and after, bias-related incidents and hate crimes soared.

Cooper's third criterion: Using all that harvested emotion for political gain. Again, what politician doesn't? Trump famously bragged that his supporters were so ardent, *"I could stand in the middle of Fifth Avenue and shoot somebody and I wouldn't lose voters."*

Which brings us to the fourth criterion: Breaking the rules of governance in the name of the people. As Cooper observed with eerie prescience:

"The demagogue always puts the people before the constitution and the laws, in face of the obvious truth that the people have placed the constitution and the laws before themselves."

Or, as eminent political theorist Hannah Arendt saw back in 1951:

"Would-be totalitarian rulers usually start their careers by boasting of their past crimes and carefully outlining their future ones."

If Trump did not actually break the law, he clearly was proud of outsmarting it, owning up to ducking taxes, greasing politicians, and much more. Supporters praised this as truth telling, which it was. The system was rigged, but he knew how to game it. And now he would game it for us.

Which explains why so many of the rest of us are still reeling. We also knew the system was rigged. But once the bad behavior was exposed, the guilty were supposed to *pay the consequences*, at least in the court of public opinion. That Trump's misconduct actually would help vault him to the White House was inconceivable.

Once again, the so-called carnival barker seized a mallet and smashed an essential stereotype: that our democracy was based on a set of common values. Another pillar of our delicate reality was shattered.

Here are two more that toppled, bringing the temple down:

First, the idea that *most citizens participate in the democratic system*. We knew that to be false, given the nation's pitifully low voter turnout, but somehow we believed it anyway. This illusion was fostered by political media that relied too much on polls to tell the story. When most of the reporting is built around projected voter numbers, it drowns out the stories about what people actually believe.

In fact, the polls were not far off, but reporters routinely overlook third-party candidates and missed the clues embedded in their numbers. Trump won many Obama voters, but Hillary Clinton lost far more of them to third parties and nonvoters. Trump didn't win even a plurality, but through the quirks of the electoral system, he won the day. The Trump team could see the possibilities. Hidebound horse race coverage blinkered the press.

The next, more consequential pillar of illusion is that "those who are politically indifferent do not matter," that they are basically neutral and constitute "no more than the inarticulate backward setting for the political life of the nation." That's a key point in Arendt's classic analysis of the rise of the Nazis and Soviet Communism, *The Origins of Totalitarianism.* (Yikes.)

Turned out, they mattered. And in their eyes, America was changing in ways that threatened their universe racially, culturally, and economically, depriving their children of the secure future that was their birthright. Meanwhile, every four years, they saw traditional candidates from both parties issue empty promises and then vanish in pursuit of secret deals.

To borrow a Marxist term, these citizens were stereotyped as *lumpen*, indifferent to "revolutionary advancement." But they were not indifferent; they were embittered. They went rogue. Arendt would have recognized it.

> ". . . The spokesmen for totalitarian movements possessed an unerring instinct for anything that ordinary party propaganda or public opinion did not care to touch. . . . The mob really believed that truth was whatever respectable society had hypocritically passed over, or covered with corruption. . . ."

Now, understandably, Arendt refers rather dismissively to Hitler's followers, who I am *not* equating with Trump's. Nevertheless the echoes of that dark era reverberate with clues to how our own reality broke. Because then, as now, facts mattered less than the fear-induced patterns that resonated with the worldview of so many.

> "The modern masses do not believe in anything visible. . . . What convinces masses are not facts, and not even invented facts, but only the consistency of the system of which they are presumably part."

Trump's system clearly was unmoored to facts. It definitely ran on the idea that the truth resided *only* in what "ordinary party propaganda" did not care to touch. Certainly, it was consistent. What's more, Trump World came complete with an alluring system of Trump Values. It was a full-service universe.

Jason Stanley, Yale professor and author of *How Propaganda Works*, described Trump Values in the *New York Times* blog The Stone:

> "In Trump's value system, nonwhites and non-Christians are the chief threats to law and order. Trump knows that reality does not call for a value-system like his; violent crime is at almost historic lows. . . . Trump is thundering about a crime wave of historic proportions, because he is an authoritarian using his speech to *define* a simple reality that legitimates his value system, leading voters to adopt it."

Trump's rhetoric underscored what his supporters already believed: that the politicians, professors, scientists, and coastal elites who wept great salt tears over immigrants and minorities didn't care about, didn't *see*, the coming catastrophe. Trump saw.

He struck a bargain, a classic authoritarian deal, with his supporters. You can bask in my favor and recognition, in the promises I make and the license I bestow, and all I ask in return is that you believe whatever I say, whenever I say it. Even when it is false. Even when it contradicts the reality of your own experience. Arendt saw that in her time, too.

> "Instead of deserting the leaders who had lied to them, they would protest that they had known all along that the statement was a lie and would admire the leaders for their superior tactical cleverness."

If I say Muslims in New Jersey celebrated when the Twin Towers fell, that the popular election was stolen, that Barack Obama bugged my campaign, even if I say the sun shone on my inaugural address, you will believe me. Or, better still, you will not care.

Because the truth is a liar.

LYING
IS THE POINT

By far the greatest source of anxiety for those watching the edifice of reality collapse is the ceaseless cascade of lies. But it is not the lies that pose the existential danger to democracy. It's the lying, the kind of thoroughgoing lying that gives rise to a whole new reality or, better still, to no reality at all.

Journalist Masha Gessen resists equating Trump with Putin, as American media are prone to do, but says they are kin in the use of the lie:

> "It's not just that both Putin and Trump lie, it is that they lie in the same way and for the same purpose—blatantly, to assert power over truth itself."

The sheer abundance of lies demonstrates, again and again, that facts are disposable, confusing devices that do not serve you, that do not matter.

So, to the question endlessly asked by an incredulous public: *Why, in the name of all that is holy, has no one confiscated Donald Trump's cell phone?* Arendt offers a partial answer in a 1974 interview:

> ". . . A lying government has constantly to rewrite its own history. On the receiving end you get not only one lie—a lie which you could go on for the rest of your days— but you get a great number of lies, depending on how the political wind blows.
>
> "And a people that no longer can believe anything cannot make up its mind. It is deprived not only of its capacity to act but also of its capacity to think and to judge. And with such a people, you can then do what you please."

One could be forgiven for believing that Trump stumbled, willy-nilly, on the authoritarian playbook because he just happened to be a charismatic narcissist, serial liar, and scenery-chewer. But if, in fact, Trump did not fully understand what he was doing, the man who followed him to the White House as "chief strategist" certainly did.

Steve Bannon, former head of the blatantly racist and mendacious news site Breitbart.com, told *The Hollywood Reporter*, before the election, that "darkness is good."

> "Dick Cheney. Darth Vader. Satan. That's power. It only helps us when they [the liberals] get it wrong. When they're blind to who we are and what we're doing."

So during the campaign and ever after, the Trump team generated swarms of outrage, absurdity, and "alternative facts," sending the media darting this way and that after shiny objects, too frantic to cull the crucial from the trivial, never pausing for the big picture that, in any case, they would not have recognized. However, many students of history did. They saw Trump not as a joke or an aberration, but as a departure, a pivot point for a country at a crossroads.

This fantastical world of unkillable lies and impotent truths arose because much of the country had accepted Trump's deal: Believe what he says, or don't and assume with a wink and a nod that you are in on the joke.

But it was a deadly serious joke, because in spurning the facts that further understanding, Trump was not merely pitching his presidency to alienated voters, he was striking at the heart of democracy itself.

In an article on ThinkProgress, Ned Resnikoff explained how:

"Consensus is the bedrock of democracy. For differences to get resolved in a properly democratic fashion, there needs to be agreement over the terms of the debate. Interlocutors must be aware of their shared rights and responsibilities, and they need to be capable of proceeding from a common set of facts and premises.

"When political actors can't agree on basic facts and procedures, compromise and rule-bound argumentation are basically impossible; politics reverts back to its natural state as a raw power struggle in which the weak are dominated by the strong."

Even if each of our realities is unique, our common cultures and environments ensure that we share some fundamental principles. That is what enables consensus, and that is what is under attack.

By degrading the very notion of shared reality, Trump has disabled the engine of democracy. As Resnikoff wrote:

> "When the truth is little more than an arbitrary personal decision, there is no common ground to be reached and no incentive to look for it."

If this truly is the goal of Team Trump, then it was staggeringly ambitious. Consider all the forces arrayed against it. Even with a stymied Congressional opposition, there remained the courts, a restive federal bureaucracy, battalions of energized activists, factions within the White House itself, and powers within the intelligence and national security communities that Trump has attacked.

As Trump bellows, they keep goring him with investigations and leaks.

As of this writing, these investigations may well prove the most effective weapon; but for Trump, who reflexively attacks any democratic institution that criticizes or constrains him, the leaks are more infuriating. They threaten his most crucial power source: public opinion. Lose that, and he deflates faster than a balloon in Macy's Thanksgiving Day Parade.

So he dominates the ether to ensure that thorny facts find no purchase there. And if he can neutralize *one* institution in particular, an institution that is *not* an institution, the rest of the resistance can probably be managed.

Clearly, the press is vulnerable. The great debates it hosted at the birth of our democracy ended long ago. In an era when the popularity of most American institutions is declining, a 2016 Gallup poll ranked TV news and newspapers just above the bottommost losers, Big Business and Congress. The media's financial state is even more tenuous. Certainly, news outlets were not spoiling for a fight that lost advertisers or invited lawsuits.

During the campaign, the mainstream media loved reporting on Trump. He made great copy and boosted audience, and his rising poll numbers made him legitimate news. But later, the liberal media lamented missing the bigger picture. They could not see it because their view was blocked by stereotypes based on past experience and validated by their echo chambers. Once Trump was nominated, they quickly corrected course and dug into his statements, his businesses, and his past.

Every president and every prospective president since Jefferson has chafed against an adversarial press doing what comes naturally. But never quite like this. Trump fired his first salvos on reporters from the campaign trail.

Atkinson, New Hampshire: *"They're horrible people. They are so illegitimate. . . ."*

Mt. Pleasant, South Carolina: *"Absolute scum. Remember that. Scum. Scum. . . ."*

Grand Rapids, Michigan: *"I would never kill 'em, but I do hate 'em. . . ."*

The attacks intensified after he won the election. Finally, on February, 16, 2017, he called a press conference to issue his proclamation of war:

"I'm making this presentation directly to the American people . . . because many of our nation's reporters and folks will not tell you the truth. . . ."

"If we don't talk about it, we are doing a tremendous disservice to the American people . . . because the press, honestly, is out of control. . . ."

"How does the press get this information that's classified? . . . It's an illegal process, and the press should be ashamed of themselves. . . ."

"The New York Times wrote a big, long, front-page story yesterday. . . . It's a joke. . . . Russia is fake news. This is fake news put out by the media. . . ."

"The Wall Street Journal . . . did a story today that was almost as disgraceful as the failing New York Times' story yesterday.

"I watch CNN. It's so much anger and hatred. . . . The public gets it. . . . They start screaming at CNN. They want to throw their placards at CNN. . . ."

And so on. The reviews of his appearance were predictably mixed.

CNN's Jake Tapper called it "wild . . . unhinged."

Fox News's Bill O'Reilly called it "bold and fresh."

The president tweeted a summary of his remarks the next day:

@realDonaldTrump
The FAKE NEWS media (failing @nytimes, @NBCNews, @ABC, @CBS, @CNN) is not my enemy, it is the enemy of the American People!

Trump is drawn to catchy phrases whatever their provenance, but this one inspired a brief shiver, since "enemy of the people" was the phrase Hitler applied to Jews, Mao to the educated class, and Stalin to almost everyone. It was a clear statement of where Trump stood. He had declared that there was no free press in his America, and no reason for one.

February 18, 2017: *"They have their own agenda and their agenda is not your agenda!"*

In this, he took shrewd advantage of a situation he had no hand in creating. There had long been one media filter for liberals and one for conservatives. Before he arrived, the nation was already seeing double.

@realDonaldTrump
Any negative polls are fake news, just like the CNN, ABC, NBC polls in the election.

The confusion generated by the Trump fog machine is truly awe-inspiring, because its messages seep into and leech the clarity from even the sturdiest of minds. Ned Resnikoff described to *On the Media* what happened to *Washington Post* reporter Ben Terris in March 2016, when Corey Lewandowski, Trump campaign manager, violently shoved Breitbart reporter Michelle Fields. Ben Terris saw it and reported it.

RESNIKOFF: What happened afterwards was the campaign and many of the campaign supporters just came down on him incredibly hard.

You know, Ben Terris is a professional reporter and one of the things Trump has been very effective at using against reporters is our sometimes natural inclination to scrutinize our own perception, just to make sure that we're not getting anything wrong. And so they used that against him. They just aggressively denied from the very beginning that this had ever happened. They just said, no, no, no.

Terris was asked over and over again by his own editors, are you sure that's what you saw, and at some point he started to doubt his own perception. And then the video came out confirming exactly what Terris had said had happened, and the Trump team just pivoted.

Terris *saw* it happen, but adrift in a boiling sea of denial, for a brief moment, he wasn't sure. In such circumstances, an honest person can lose his mind a little.

Trump's use of the epithet serves a similar purpose: Crooked Hillary. Little Marco. Crazy Bernie. Fake Tears Chuck Schumer. Failing *New York Times*. Like musical earworms, they carve pathways in the brain. They take up residence, breed associations, breed doubt.

Trump's twitter finger taps out a dissonant melody and cranks it up to eleven to drown out reality. It's stupefying.

America is so very noisy these days.

RECOVERING REALITY

American history is pocked with ferment, battles, and brawls over what is true. But at this moment, the nation seems to be waging civil war over reality itself. It is thrilling to watch, and tough to sit out, because the stakes are so high. But how will it end? Arendt suggests that demagogues have a fatal vulnerability: "The deceivers started with self-deception."

Trump is briefed daily, but judging from his speeches and tweets, the information he retains comes mainly from Fox News, Breitbart, a conspiracy website called Infowars, and a close circle of confidants. His comments suggest that he watches the other cable and network news shows and reads the *New York Times* and *Wall Street Journal*, mostly to get angry.

"Oddly enough, the only person likely to be an ideal victim of complete manipulation is the President of the United States," said Arendt.

> "Because of the immensity of his job, he must surround himself with advisers . . . who exercise their power chiefly by filtering the information that reaches the President and by interpreting the outside world for him."

So Trump will cite a number and respond to a reporter's correction by saying "people told me." He'll refer to a terrorist attack in, say, Sweden, and rebut that nation's stunned objections by saying it was on Fox News. Arendt argued that the walls of such a bunker must collapse eventually.

> "The self-deceived deceiver loses all contact with not only his audience, but also the real world, which still will catch up with him, because he can remove his mind from it but not his body."

We'll see how that goes.

Meanwhile, since the election, the fact-based media have engaged in some long-overdue soul-searching. One fateful error now conceded: From the moment Trump emerged, reporters should have laughed less and reported more. As Michael Signer told *On the Media* during the 2016 campaign:

SIGNER: My study of demagogues shows that satire does not work. . . . When you lampoon him or when you satirize him or when you call him a clown or a carnival barker, none of that matters because they're showmen, and they . . . connect with people in a way that ordinary mortals do not. . . . Actually taking a demagogue seriously in their claims and educating the audience about how . . . what they're doing actually hurts the country . . . that's what the history of successful confrontation with demagogues has shown.

ME: You are optimistic that the American people will overcome what you suggest could be an existential threat to the nation. Why? You're not going to invoke American Exceptionalism, are you?

SIGNER: Ohhh. I am. [*laughs*] I wasn't going to, but you got me. Demagogues thrive when we're cynical about truth. They start to deflate when we put faith back again in public reason, and if you look at the history, we have always prevailed. And it's not the checks and balances that we have . . . it's because the American people in the end always choose that demagogues are beneath them.

Signer must have found election day a great disappointment. But on the bright side, it provoked a mobilization, the likes of which few Americans can remember, among the public and the press.

Politico's Jack Shafer, a longtime press critic, sees Trump's hostility toward the media as a liberation, "because all the old scripts that go into the formula of making political news have to be completely rethought."

Example: the formula that trades *access* for a degree of self-censorship. Traditionally, reporters cultivate powerful White House sources whom they can call when they need a quote. But if those sources are upset by something the reporters write, they won't pick up the phone. The reporters must have those quotes, no matter how bland and predictable, to finish their stories; so to keep the quotes coming, they may leave out some juicy facts. For the public, this is a terrible deal.

Now the rules have changed. The White House abounds with official quotes, but too often they are, in the parlance of Richard Nixon's press secretary Ron Ziegler, "inoperative," meaning "false." Now the customary animus between the White House and the press, dating back to John Adams and seething under Nixon, is boiling over.

But this time, the press has some powerful allies. Factions within the Congress, the White House, and the entire federal bureaucracy are leaking like lobster pots. And it's pure gold.

Speaking of Richard Nixon, Shafer told *On the Media* the Trump era may spawn a new golden age for journalism, just as Nixon's did, because, like Nixon, Trump has waved a red flag in front of what has long been a narcotized bull.

SHAFER: Both Nixon and his leading surrogate, Spiro Agnew, were intensely hostile and critical of the press. They thought that the press had overstepped its bounds . . . they thought the press should just provide a stenographic exercise. Instead, the press basically threw off the complacency that maybe it had fallen into in the Fifties and in the early Sixties and saw Nixon's abuses of power, in part, because the Nixon Administration *was* so hostile to the press.

SHAFER: Reporters are like red ants. If you leave red ants alone, you probably have no problem; but if you kick a red anthill, you've got a swarm of angry, biting insects. . . . You show me a politician who made a lifelong practice of attacking the press, you show me where those political careers end.

ME: You think this could all not only set journalists' missions straight but actually help revitalize the struggling industry.

SHAFER: Trump has driven readers and viewers to newspapers and television across the board. Wherever he goes, he makes news. But it won't always be the news that he's looking for, and wherever there's conflict, readers follow. . . . They want to see conflict, they want to see bloodshed, because that's, you know, the day-to-day experience of our life. It's war out there, Brooke!

The mainstream media have recovered some of that old revolutionary fire. The current crisis seems to have blocked the reflex to protect the appearance of objectivity at all costs by giving equal time to unequal arguments and to preserve numerical "balance" at the cost of misleading the public.

In this new reality there would be far less mincing of words and pulling of punches. Information. Investigation. Clarity. The Washington reporter turned war reporter, with a sense of purpose intensified by the danger.

On to glory and the grave! Would Lippmann laugh, cheer, or . . . cry?

> "If the newspapers . . . are to be charged with the duty of translating the whole public life of mankind, so that every adult can arrive at an opinion on every moot topic . . . they are bound to fail . . . they will continue to fail."

Lippmann would be confounded by media in the third millennium—except for the part about people not paying for news; that would seem very familiar. (Recently, though, Trump's rise has moved many people to view paying for news as a moral obligation, an act of resistance. It may not last, and if it doesn't, journalism probably will fail again.)

But Lippmann would not recognize a world with a printing press in every pocket; where media's age-old gatekeepers are trampled by what PressThink's Jay Rosen dubbed "the people formerly known as the audience."

In this world, professional journalists are distinguished from the audience only by how well they use their hard-earned skills, experience, and expertise. If they can't dive into the quicksand of conflicting narratives now devouring the earth and extract what's important, they might as well go down with it.

In fact, we *all* need new skills for that, because in Trump World, traditional media are routinely bypassed. He delivers most of his points unmediated, fresh, and fun-sized, straight to your screen via Twitter. Yet those 140-character epistles are far more complex, more layered, than they seem. To grasp the messages beneath, the subtlety of the manipulation, you must understand Trump's method. You have to learn his code. SAD!

To help you master Trumpspeak, we offer the following Taxonomy of Trump Tweets, devised by cognitive linguist George Lakoff.

Category One: PREEMPTIVE FRAMING

> @realDonaldTrump
> Only reason the hacking of the poorly
> defended DNC is discussed is that the loss
> by the Dems was so big that they are totally
> embarrassed!

The idea here, Lakoff says, "is to frame an issue before other people get a chance to, to put the idea out there first."

So how did Trump frame the narrative in this tweet?

First, he claims that the hacking of the Democratic National Committee is not, in itself, worthy of discussion. Second, he says "the Dems lost big," when in fact Hillary Clinton won the popular vote and lost the Electoral College by a slim margin. Third, he implies that the Republican National Committee was better defended, even though the RNC also was hacked by the Russians (only, they didn't leak any of *that* stuff).

So there are three distinct, preemptive distortions of reality in one itty-bitty tweet. This guy's *good*.

Category Two: THE DIVERSION TWEET

@realDonaldTrump

The cast and producers of Hamilton, which I hear is highly overrated, should immediately apologize to Mike Pence for their terrible behavior

The diversion tweet is used to provoke the mainstream media with an outburst, often related to cultural or social issues, that fills a news cycle with shock or sneers and diverts attention from a far more important story. This tweet, slamming the cast for reading Mike Pence a statement when he attended the show, overshadowed the news that Trump paid out $25 million to settle lawsuits against Trump University for fraud.

Category Three: THE TRIAL BALLOON

@realDonaldTrump

The United States must greatly strengthen and expand its nuclear capability until such time as the world comes to its senses regarding nukes

This is pretty much self-explanatory. As Lakoff explains, "He's going to see how people react to this, and then he'll know what to do in the future. People were confused; they talked about nuclear proliferation a little bit and then it went away."

Category Four: THE DEFLECTION TWEET

@realDonaldTrump

Just cannot believe a judge would put our country in such peril. If something happens blame him and court system. People pouring in. Bad!

@realDonaldTrump

The so-called angry crowds in home districts of some Republicans are actually, in numerous cases, planned out by liberal activists. Sad!

@realDonaldTrump

The real scandal here is that classified information is illegally given out by "intelligence" like candy. Very un-American!

This is Trump's clear favorite, whereby he dodges responsibility, usually by blaming the messenger. Every tweet about the media falls into this category.

Naturally, he applies these techniques to his spoken remarks as well. This is how he embeds his reality. If his reality is not your reality, resist the temptation to repost his missives. *Reposting only reinforces them.* Instead, note them, mark them, and you will be better equipped to hang on to your own.

Having decoded his tweets and speeches, it would be wiser not to dwell on them too much. In times of stress, there's no point spiking your cortisol levels by fulminating on petty lies, tantrums, or hypocrisies. (Why rage that Melania Trump, in her youth, may have violated Trump's immigration policies if you don't like those policies anyway?) Preserve your outrage for issues that reflect your values. Reserve your strength.

⇄

This is the part of the book that actually can make you feel a little better. Meaningful action is a time-tested treatment for moral panic.

Focus on policies that matter to you. Congressional offices keep tallies of phone calls from their districts. Make calls. As for street protests, they feel great, but unless they are large and well planned, they're not all that effective. Since the president actually may believe the polls are rigged, even the most exemplary protests are unlikely to move his needle.

But protests do raise funds. When the American Civil Liberties Union showed up at airports to assist travelers caught in Trump's travel ban, it garnered six times the donations in a single weekend that it usually gets in a year. And they do spook legislators, especially in their districts.

Protests also have another impact: They transform observers into activists. As Brian Resnick of *Vox* wrote, "If people who are showing up to protests just because they are curious and sympathetic eventually move on to greater, more consistent action, the movement grows. And change can happen."

But not soon, and not without sustained effort. Action is vital. Democratic progress stalls without that eternal tug-of-war. But activism alone does not address the bigger issue, the focus of this tract. You cannot march to a long-term solution to your reality problem with a cadre of like-minded allies. That is a solitary journey, and it never ends. You have to travel out of your universe into the universe of others, and leave your old map at home.

THE RECKONING

This is the essence of all sciences—that you should know who you will be when the Day of Reckoning arrives.

—Rumi

The day will come. Oh yes! Mark my words, Seinfeld. Your day of reckoning is coming, when an evil wind will blow through your little play world and wipe that smug smile off your face. And I'll be there, in all my glory, watching, watching as it all comes crumbling down.

—Newman

was thinking of *Gulliver's Travels*, Jonathan Swift's gloriously brutal evisceration of eighteenth-century England. I got stuck on two of the strange species Gulliver met on his way, wondering if they might serve as workable metaphors today.

Consider the contorted Laputans, philosophers of science who live on an island floating in the sky. Literally they cannot see straight.

> "Their heads were all reclined, either to the right, or the left; one of their eyes turned inward, and the other directly up to the zenith. . . .
>
> "It seems the minds of these people are so taken up with intense speculations, that they neither can speak nor attend to the discourses of others . . ."

So they hire "flappers," who use a bladder to gently strike the mouth of the man who is to speak and the ear of the one who is to listen.

"This flapper is likewise employed diligently to attend his master in his walks, and upon occasion to give him a soft flap on his eyes; because he is always so wrapped up in cogitation, that he is in manifest danger of falling down every precipice, and bouncing his head against every post; and in the streets, of justling others, or being justled himself into the kennel."

Laputans, floating free above as their king tyrannizes the people below, excel at theoretical mathematics but find basic geometry vulgar, so they produce lopsided buildings and ill-fitting clothes. Snugly immersed in their rarefied musings and self-regard, they are oblivious to the results. Laputans are, at the same time, quite brilliant and incorrigibly stupid.

Next, the Houyhnhnms. They represent a less barbed, more confounding critique of blinkered reality. As it happens, the Houyhnhnms are horses, governed purely by reason. They need neither rulers, nor money, nor even a word that means "lying." Because their universe is built on a common foundation of observable facts, they never disagree.

Gulliver reveres the Houyhnhnms and wants to spend his life among them, but they cast him out. Despite his skills and congenial nature, clearly he is of the Yahoo race, that of depraved, grunting, feral humanoids who rob and kill each other and despoil the world. Gulliver loathes his kinship to the depraved Yahoo.

Where the hell are you going with this, I hear you cry. (Getting there.)

When Gulliver returns to England, he sees only the detestable Yahoo in his family and friends, and he is not wrong. He now sees the human race with painful clarity. Yet still he misses the bigger picture, because he doesn't reflect on those moments among the Houyhnhnms when he actually flinched a bit—when, for instance, they traded their offspring to one another, or went off to die without reflecting, even for a moment, on the lives they had lived.

The Houyhnhnms do not love or yearn, or doubt or mourn. They have no art, no imagination. They base their codes only on what they see, and nothing else exists.

Facts can address the visible world, but not the world unseen. Humans are incapable of separating one from the other, because we can't live without a bigger reality, an encompassing truth, which we can't construct without weaving the seen and unseen together. That's because, as I proposed at the start of all this, facts and truth are not the same.

If they were, then two rational people, after pooling and verifying each other's evidence, would come to the same conclusions, right? They would revise their views to fit the facts. But there never are two rational people. There is only one. And it is me. My facts are correct.

If you think I am cracking wise to make a point, you are mistaken. I am sincere. My facts reflect the world as it is. Donald Trump's facts, as a rule, do not. I do not know the facts of his supporters; not really. I only know they voted for Trump, which is inconceivable to me.

Which is to say, I cannot conceive of it.

And maybe that is a place to begin the reckoning.

Our facts are incomplete, our truth limited. I concede that, while fully expecting that new information poses no fundamental threat to my reality. At worst, I will have to tweak it, as little as possible, just as William James described.

Indeed, I am so certain of that, I can safely venture out to take in a few new sights, a few new facts, to start to figure out what's going on *out there*. Because not knowing is much scarier than knowing. Give me a diagnosis, even if it's terminal, because I already think it is.

Okay, political turmoil is a chronic condition, but life is terminal, so I might as well get on with managing the pain.

⇆

"Remember Democracy never lasts long. It soon wastes exhausts and murders itself. There never was a Democracy Yet, that did not commit suicide. It is in vain to Say that Democracy is less vain, less proud, less selfish, less ambitious or less avaricious than Aristocracy or Monarchy. . . . Those Passions are the same in all Men under all forms of Simple Government, and when unchecked, produce the same Effects of Fraud Violence and Cruelty. . . . Individuals have conquered themselves, Nations and large Bodies of Men, never."

—*From John Adams to John Taylor,*
December 17, 1814

Listen to the angry man. He says democracy is merely a template, a structure as prone to human frailty as any other. Yet it remains our stereotype, the hallmark of our superiority, passed down from the founders who clearly had their own doubts about it, and not just Adams, but also Hamilton and, to a lesser extent, Madison. They doubted because they knew that in the final analysis, we are not Swift's hyper-rational horses (though Jefferson thought we had the potential).

Mostly they saw in us some measure of Yahoo, now and forever.

Individuals conquer themselves, said Swift, said Huxley, said Adams. Individuals also can surpass themselves.

Either way, we have subscribed as a nation to that democratic code. Unless we are ready to leave it in the dust, our obligation as citizens is to repair and improve the nation in which we live. Lippmann warned that whenever realities collide there is fallout, in the form of disillusion and cynicism, and it devours what is good along with the bad. So it is our turn, as individuals, to test the soundness of that code.

There are countless actions to take, but all such efforts are hobbled, inexorably, by rage, bafflement, and despair. So to defend against all that emotional interference, I'm making a case for taking a stab at a little transcendence, not to compromise principles of justice and equality, but to expand the world that, for so long, has, in Lippmann's words, fit us as snugly as an old shoe.

Speaking as a reporter who has worked abroad and in places just as foreign to me in America (hailing as I do from the impervious bubble of Brooklyn), and who has had a lot of strange conversations, I believe *there is a path*, probably not to agreement, but to comprehension. Finding that path lowers your blood pressure so you can work; it also helps you map the territory *you* must travel.

No one else can deliver you from reality trouble, not Jesus, Allah, Yahweh, Brahman, Quetzalcoatl, scientific reasoning, or random chance.

But the price is very high. It's rational to conclude that it is not worth the considerable trouble and time required to venture forth, to protest, to doubt, to listen, to change others, or to be changed.

Personally, I wouldn't blame you, whatever you choose to do or not do. It is possible that, after just a few bad years, all this horror, the terrible mystery of it, will slowly sink beneath our carefully curated horizons from whence it came.

But we can't simply retreat back into our own realities after what we've seen. Though we are quite adept at not seeing, *unseeing* is an altogether different matter. We experienced reality crash. Now our reality is going to need some tweaking.

Facts are real and will reassert themselves eventually. In order to repair our reality, we need more of them, from people and places we do not see. Just watching the walleyed would-be Laputans in the White House, designing unworkable structures and falling down holes, offers a cautionary tale of what happens when we blind ourselves to facts.

To repeat Arendt, eventually the real world catches up with us all.

But we cannot see the real world, whatever that may be. We live in the world that we made from what we see and what we know, and also in the world that we didn't make and do not see and do not know.

We are Yahoo. We struggle in them both.

People in every world share that struggle, though they may not see it that way.

I see it—just the awareness of it—as a path like the chambered spiral of a nautilus shell, always unwinding, spinning us in wider and wider circles, far from where we started. Along the way, there are flashes and illuminations, but no clarity and no end.

We Yahoo can't get there from here. We breed infinite realities and they never can be reconciled. We cannot fully enter someone else's. But if we really look, we might actually *see* that other reality reflected in that person's eyes, and therein lies the beginning of the end of our reality problem.

SOURCES

Adams, John to John Taylor, December 17, 1814. *Founders Online*, National Archives, last modified December 28, 2016, http://founders.archives.gov/documents/Adams/99-02-02-6371.

Arendt, Hannah. "Hannah Arendt: From an Interview." *New York Review of Books*, October 26, 1978.

———. *The Origins of Totalitarianism*. New York: Houghton Mifflin Harcourt, 1973.

Cooper, James Fenimore. "The American Democrat: Or, Hints on the Social and Civic Relations of the United States of America." Originally published 1838 by H. & E. Phinney.

Dick, Philip K. "How to Build a Universe That Doesn't Fall Apart Two Days Later" in *The Shifting Realities of Philip K. Dick: Selected Literary and Philosophical Writings*. Edited by Lawrence Sutin. New York: Vintage, 1996.

DiNatale, Sara and Maria Sacchetti. "South Boston Brothers Allegedly Beat Homeless Man." *Boston Globe*, August 19, 2015. https://www.bostonglobe.com/metro/2015/08/19/homeless/iTagewS4bnvBKWxxPvFcAJ/story.html.

Dowd, Maureen. "Liberties; Living la Vida Trumpa." *New York Times*. November 17, 1999. http://www.nytimes.com/1999/11/17/opinion/liberties-living-la-vida-trumpa.html.

Eagelman, David M. "The Umwelt." *Edge*. https://www.edge.org/response-detail/11498.

Gallup Poll. "Confidence in Institutions." http://www.gallup.com/poll/1597/confidence-institutions.aspx.

Gessen, Masha, interview by Brooke Gladstone. "Masha Gessen on the 'Impulse to Normalize.'" *On the Media*, podcast audio, December 2, 2016, http://www.wnyc.org/story/masha-gessen-impulse-normalize/.

———. "The Putin Paradigm." *New York Review of Books*, December 13, 2016. http://www.nybooks.com/daily/2016/12/13/putin-paradigm-how-trump-will-rule/.

Healy, Melissa. "Why Conservatives Are More Likely Than Liberals to Believe False Information About Threats." *LA Times*. March 28, 2017. http://www.latimes.com/science/sciencenow/la-sci-sn-conservative-believe-false-threats-20170202-story.html.

James, William. "What Pragmatism Means," in *Pragmatism: A New Name for Some Old Ways of Thinking*. New York: Longman Green and Co, 1907.

Jefferson, Thomas. "Virginia Statute on Religious Freedom." Originally published 1786.

Lakoff, George, interview by Brooke Gladstone. "A Taxonomy of Trump Tweets." *On the Media*, podcast audio, January 13, 2017, http://www.wnyc.org/story/taxonomy-trump-tweets/.

Le Guin, Ursula K. *The Left Hand of Darkness*. New York: Ace, 1987.

Lewandowsky, Stephan, Klaus Oberauer, and Gilles Gignac. "NASA Faked the Moon Landing—Therefore (Climate) Science Is a Hoax." *Psychological Science*, 24, no. 5 (2013). http://websites.psychology.uwa.edu.au/labs/cogscience/documents/LskyetalPsychScienceinPressClimateConspiracy.pdf.

Lippmann, Walter. *Public Opinion*. New York: Harcourt, Brace and Company, 1922.

Miller, Joanne M., Kyle L. Saunders, and Christina E. Farhart. "Conspiracy Endorsement as Motivated Reasoning: The Moderating Roles of Political Knowledge and Trust." *American Journal of Political Science* 60, no. 4 (2016): 824–844. doi: 10.1111/ajps.12234.

Milton, John. "Areopagitica: A Speech for the Liberty of Unlicensed Printing to the Parliament of England." Originally published 1644. Project Gutenberg. http://www.gutenberg.org/files/608/608-h/608-h.htm.

Postman, Neil. *Amusing Ourselves to Death: Public Discourse in the Age of Show Business*. 20 anv. ed. New York: Penguin, 2005.

Resnik, Brian. "4 Rules for Making a Protest Work, According to Experts." Vox. January 31, 2017. http://www.vox.com/policy-and-politics/2017/1/31/14430584/protest-trump-strategies-experts.

Resnikoff, Ned. "Trump's Lies Have a Purpose. They Are an Assault on Democracy." ThinkProgress.org. November 27, 2016. https://think progress.org/when-everything-is-a-lie-power-is-the-only-truth -1e641751d150#.rmdsy4d4m.

———, interview by Brooke Gladstone. "Trump's Reality Distortion Field." *On the Media*, podcast audio, January 13, 2017. http://www.wnyc.org/story/trumps-reality-distortion-field/.

Schopenhauer, Arthur. *The Essays of Arthur Schopenhauer: Studies in Pessimism*. Translated by T. Bailey Saunders. Project Gutenberg, 2004. https://www.gutenberg.org/files/10732/10732-8.txt

Shafer, Jack, interview by Brooke Gladstone. "How Trump Might Shape the Media He So Despises." *On the Media*, podcast audio, January 20, 2017. http://www.wnyc.org/story/how-trump-might-save -media-he-so-despises/.

Signer, Michael. *Demagogue: The Fight to Save America from Its Worst Enemies*. New York: St. Martin's Press, 2009.

———. "The Electoral College Was Created to Stop Demagogues Like Trump." *Time*. November 17, 2016. http://time.com /4575119/electoral-college-demagogues/.

———, interview by Brooke Gladstone. "So You've Got a Demagogue." *On the Media*, podcast audio, December 11, 2015. http://www.wnyc.org/story/so-youve-got-demagogue/.

Southern Poverty Law Center. "Update: 1,094 Bias-Related Incidents in the Month Following the Election." December 16, 2016. https://www .splcenter.org/hatewatch/2016/12/16/update-1094-bias-related-incidents -month-following-election.

Stanley, Jason. "Beyond Lying: Donald Trump's Authoritarian Reality." The Stone (blog), *New York Times*. November 4, 2016. https://www.ny times.com/2016/11/05/opinion/beyond-lying-donald-trumps-authoritarian -reality.html.

Swift, Jonathan. *Gulliver's Travels*. Reprint of the 1892 George Bell and Sons edition by David Price, Project Gutenberg, 2009. https://www .gutenberg.org/files/829/829-h/829-h.htm.